The Fireside Book

A picture and a poem
for every mood
chosen by

David Hope

Printed and published by
D.C. THOMSON & CO., LTD.,
185 Fleet Street, LONDON EC4A 2HS.

ISBN 1-84535-049-9

SNOWDROPS

AS a child
I waited for the snowdrops,
watching through the Winter
for their joy.
Every Spring
beneath the maple tree,
they poked bright heads
through icy grass.
Their dance
called me out of doors
to greet on bended knee
a waking earth.

Rachel Wallace-Oberle

APRIL

S		2	9	16	23	30
M		3	10	17	24	—
Tu		4	11	18	25	—
W		5	12	19	26	—
Th		6	13	20	27	—
F		7	14	21	28	—
S	1	8	15	22	29	—

MAY

S	—	7	14	21	28
M	1	8	15	22	29
Tu	2	9	16	23	30
W	3	10	17	24	31
Th	4	11	18	25	—
F	5	12	19	26	—
S	6	13	20	27	—

JUNE

S	—	4	11	18	25
M	—	5	12	19	26
Tu	—	6	13	20	27
W	—	7	14	21	28
Th	1	8	15	22	29
F	2	9	16	23	30
S	3	10	17	24	—

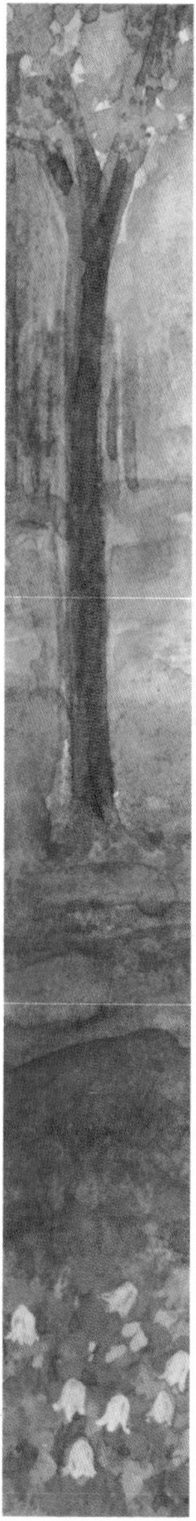

CONTENTS

THE FIRST DAY

I WISH I could remember the first day,
First hour, first moment of your meeting me;
If bright or dim the season it might be;
Summer or Winter for aught I can say.
So, unrecorded did it slip away,
So blind was I to see and to foresee,
So dull to mark the budding of my tree
That would not blossom, yet, for many a May.

If only I could recollect it! Such
A day of days! I let it come and go
As traceless as a thaw of bygone snow.
It seemed to mean so little, meant so much!
If only now I could recall that touch,
First touch of hand in hand! —
Did one but know!

Christina Rossetti

WILD GOOSE CHASE

ALL that bright February day
we had sought them,
Among the lone fields —
The gale-swept woods.
Then with the swiftness
of a thrown spear
They rose — from the far corner
of a marsh;
Streamlined in grey — wings glinting —
necks outstretched —
Their wild music ringing
loud and clear:
Grey geese! Sound ever in my heart
your trumpets harsh.

John Niven

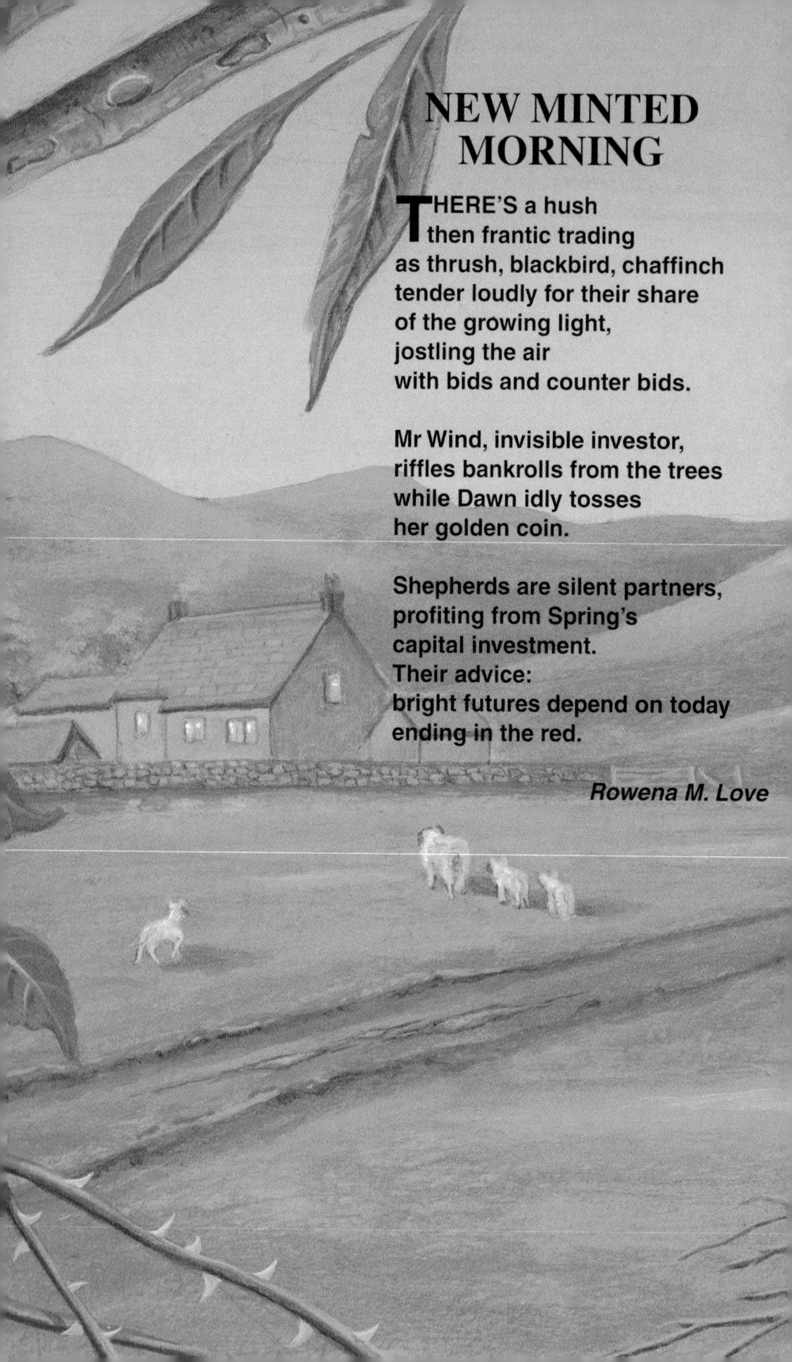

NEW MINTED MORNING

THERE'S a hush
then frantic trading
as thrush, blackbird, chaffinch
tender loudly for their share
of the growing light,
jostling the air
with bids and counter bids.

Mr Wind, invisible investor,
riffles bankrolls from the trees
while Dawn idly tosses
her golden coin.

Shepherds are silent partners,
profiting from Spring's
capital investment.
Their advice:
bright futures depend on today
ending in the red.

Rowena M. Love

KING-CUPS ON A BARROW

WEATHER-WORN old woman with your
blossom-laden barrow,
Are you April in disguise, those precious
wares to bring?
Who but she could offer me, in
streets so drab and narrow,
The shining gold that lies on
sunlit meadows in the Spring!

Choose me not your daffodils —
though sleek they are and slender:
Not your gay anemones nor lilac
all ablow:
Nor will I buy your tulips, for all
their rosy splendour:
But sell me of your king-cups,
from the meadows that I know!

Back at home they'll tell me of
the cuckoo-flowers adorning
Meads where thorn and willow-tree
are breaking as of old!
Shall I wait or hesitate upon an
April morning
To change a little silver coin for
such a wealth of gold?

Glynfab John

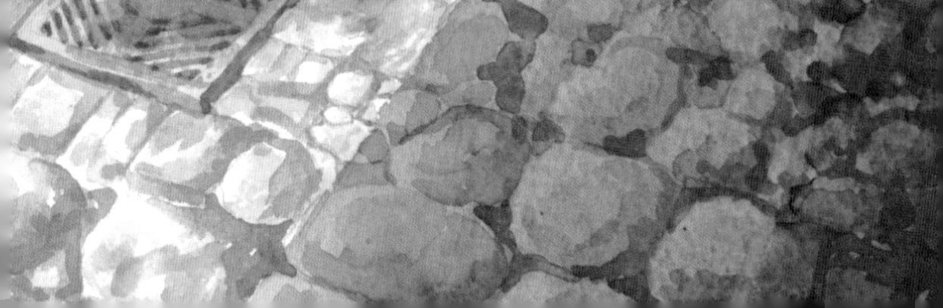

BLACKBIRD IN SPRING

FOLLOW the sound. You'll find him
on the crown of the roof, centre stage
for an alto tenor, boosted

to the left, to the right,
by bunches of pink and white blossom.
Puffing up in the encroaching chill

of evening, watch him give
his audience of one, perhaps more,
a full and protean repertoire —

— Springtime cantata for one chorister.

Ian Nimmo White

AT BLUEBELL TIME

IT was the sun that tempted me
Across a rustic stile,
Free as a bird, and aimlessly
Walking an extra mile,
Into the woodlands bursting green,
Where bluebells' silky heads
Were bidding me to step between
Their lovely dew-laced beds,
To fill my nostrils with the scent
Oozing from rain-washed trees,
And keep it there, for moments spent
In memory of these.

Alice Jean Don

OUT OF THE PAST

THE chalky bones of Norman knights
Lie crumbling in the mould,
Where once the din of battle roused
The green and peaceful wold.

Nine hundred years have passed away
Since gallant lords rode by —
Yet ghostly horsemen haunt this field
When twilight dims the sky.

Then, from their shrouds of mystery,
The heroes of the strife,
Who fought and fell in bloodier days,
As phantoms come to life.

They charge till dawn on fiery steeds,
Their ancient foes to rout,
For night is spent — and mortals stir —
Ere spectral wars fade out.

But now I watch the tractor bleed
And freely shed its lime —
To serve our deathless fellow-clay,
Here grey as hoary Time.

O Earth, be green and fruitful soon,
Bestow the gift of bread;
And every ear of wheat shall hear
The whispers of the dead.

Glynfab John

CLARSACH

THEY had scarcely noticed her before.
A slip of a thing no more than sixteen,
A glitter of eyes and auburn hair —
It was November and they wanted nothing
But the peat fire and a whiskied head.
That first night she played the heads turned,
Fell away from their loose talk;
One by one they heard a rippling
Like the shudder of breeze over the black loch,
Like the unfurling of swans.
It was her hands —
The grace and flow of the fingers
Playing with the taut stems of the strings.
They saw their own hands then,
Lumped and ruddy, knuckled with fights.
She played them quiet. Like a long wave
She washed them ashore to the island
Where she wanted them, beached them
Dry and wondering, dog-eyed,
In the long echo that was left
behind.

Kenneth C. Steven

OUR VILLAGE STORE

IF you have the time to spare,
Will you come with me and share,
The wonders of our village store?
With pots of honey by the door,
Shelves on shelves of sweets in jars,
That seem to reach up to the stars,
Shortbread biscuits in square tins,
Flour stored in silvered bins,
Brooms and mops and spades and forks,
Writing paper, coloured chalks,
Screws and nails and brass door handles,
Christmas lights and tallow candles,
Nuts and raisins, candied peeling,
Home cured hams hung from the ceiling,
Such a feast of magic spells,
Mingled with enticing smells,
And, what's more, on top of that,
There's time to have a friendly chat,
Such is the charm of country lore,
Embodied in our village store.

Brian H. Gent

SHE WALKS IN BEAUTY

SHE walks in beauty, like the night
Of cloudless climes and starry skies;
And all that's best of dark and bright
Meet in her aspect and her eyes:
Thus mellow'd to that tender light
Which heaven to gaudy day denies.

One shade the more, one ray the less,
Had half impair'd the nameless grace
Which waves in every raven tress,
Or softly lightens o'er her face;
Where thoughts serenely sweet express
How pure, how dear their dwelling-place.

And on that cheek, and o'er that brow,
So soft, so calm, yet eloquent,
The smiles that win, the tints that glow,
But tell of days in goodness spent,
A mind at peace with all below,
A heart whose love is innocent!

Lord Byron

MOONLIGHT AND DREAMS

THE moon sends down her kisses
And bathes me in her light,
For I'm not one who misses
The wonders of the night.

And when a cloud impinges
On her celestial place,
She smiles through wispy fringes
Caught up in her embrace.

She leads me to the ocean
Where beams through ripples dart,
And fills me with emotion
Whilst winds enslave my heart.

And then I know for certain,
Above the tidal streams,
Mysterious as night's curtain,
She titillates my dreams.

Alice Jean Don

EVENING DUSK

A LONESOME bird with plaintive cry
Speeds on its homeward flight,
As twilight silently descends
And slowly fades to night.
The soft air holds the balmy scent
Of jasmine, rose and musk,
And subtle fragrance seems to linger
In the evening dusk.

A wisp of smoke, a pearly moon,
The silhouettes of trees,
Sighs and muffled whisperings
Are caught up in the breeze.
Then darkness steals across the sky
And stars come out to play,
As night lets down her sequinned curtains
Of the closing day.

Kathleen Gillum

SOME JUNE DAY

WE will drive there some June day
To the furthest place west where the shell sand
Stretches in white miles till it turns to sky.
You'll take off your shoes and splash the shallows,
Joy in the flickering of fish, the dance of crabs;
You'll take my hand and tell me we should run
Fast as we can, fast till we lose our breath. And I, believing,
Will run with you, will laugh too, because of this —
The Summer and the blue, the sudden lightness of the world
Upon my shoulders. Slowly we'll come back, still out of breath,
Drive towards evening to the village for wine and shellfish —
Soft salty lips of the Atlantic —
As a huge orange moon
Peels piece by piece across the sea.

Kenneth C. Steven

BLOW GENTLY

STAY lightsome and lovely,
And whisper to me
Whilst shimmering moonbeams
Drip over the sea.
Blow gently, cool breezes,
O'er waves crawling near.
Enchant me with music
So sweet to the ear.

Blow soft little echoes
Across shapeless miles,
And bring me the magic
Of mystical isles.
Blow haunting songs soothing,
Don't ever depart
From waters enslaving
My fluttering heart.

Alice Jean Don

FLEETING MOMENTS

JUST sitting by a limpid pool,
Where zephyr breezes gently cool,
Gazing at a mountain high,
Birds gliding in a clear blue sky.

Watching salmon as they leap,
Intent their rendezvous to keep,
A field with butterflies at play,
The special scent of new-mown hay.

Bright sunlight's sparkle on the sea,
Pink blossom on an almond tree,
The tryst twixt bumble bee and rose,
A lazy day in which to doze.

Flickering candles in a church,
A cheeky robin on his perch,
Such wondrous things we all can share,
In fleeting moments waiting there.

Brian H. Gent

BARN OWL

LIKE a ballerina
Floating on cushioned air
Dressed in velvet costume
Golden-brown white
Skipping over hedgerows
And by the hillside's edge
Just faltering for a second
In Turner's light at dusk —
Then changing dainty wings
Of the dancer
For the rhythmic beats
Of the hunter's flight.

David Elder

GARDEN AT TWILIGHT

BLUE shadows blend above the dreaming earth,
Changing known shapes to dim, imagined things.
Roses toss fragrance to emergent stars,
Moths dance a minuet on silver wings.

Away among the indigo beyond
A sleeping tree sways, mute and unaware.
She stirs her leaves, yet scarcely heeds the breath
Of night birds singing love songs in her hair.

Joan Howes

DRIFTWOOD

ON East Coast, West Coast
No one knows where they go,
Whence they came,
An endless cycle of tide and time,
Oiled by the moon and gravity force.
Erosion and salt, bleach and storm
Carve their names on the spindles
And splinters of tree trunk,
Floating like flotsam in the world without aim,
Until one day the tide marks them out,
Tosses them high on the shore
And makes seafarers landlubbers
Once more.

David Elder

GENTLE NIGHT

GENTLE midnight, scented sweet
  With woodbine, you enthrall,
And quell the Summer's sultry heat
Beneath your cooling pall.

Light breezes croon among the trees,
So soothing to the ear,
And only watchful eyes can seize
The magic atmosphere.

Under the moon's delightful beams,
And stars hung out in space,
My fantasies and pleasant dreams
Are held in your embrace.

And never will these dreams be lost
Whilst I a vigil keep,
When ponds and lakes are moonlight
  glossed,
And quiet valleys sleep.

Alice Jean Don

TREASURE!

NO pirate chief was ever more
delighted by his swag,
No buccaneer more boastful of
the contents of his bag
Than Emily, her eyes alight,
her cheeks as pink as peach,
her seaside bucket heavy with
the treasures of the beach:
A tiny starfish, cast ashore,
its coral arms a-sprawl,
Some seaweed, wet and plumply brown
just rescued from a pool.
A limpet and some cockleshells,
a clutch of winkles too,
A piece of driftwood, carved and smooth,
some polished glass of blue.
Such swag which may, to other folk
seem neither rich nor rare,
To Emily, with wiser eyes,
are jewels beyond compare.

Margaret Ingall

THE LILY

LAST year we dug the pond —
Heaved up roots, old wire and pots,
Smoothed the deep ground, lined it,
Let water flow into its hold like liquid glass.
Your family gave you the lily for Christmas;
All Winter it slept in the water,
Through the fierce blue days of January,
When ice grew thick as a doorstep there
And it seemed it would be Winter for eternity.
But the year flowed slowly back in time,
Melted into the first blossom of Spring,
And the geese struggled the skies for Iceland.
We had forgotten all about the lily until,
One day, it opened its heart in the middle of the sun
Like a princess, and we marvelled, laughed, came close
In wonderment as if some baby star
Had crashed into our grass and stayed alight.
For four whole days we were like our own children
And the lily was the centre of the world.

Kenneth C. Steven

IN TWILIGHT

IN evening's silver-tinctured sheen,
The winking waters bid me walk
Along sequestered margins green,
Charmed by the songbirds' drowsy talk.

Till night unwraps her darkly pall,
And dizzy moths are just a dream,
I wallow in the bliss that falls
Around the corrugated stream.

Among the bowers, leafy bent,
The breezy minstrels softly sing,
And soothing echoes, skyward sent,
Ride on a trembling gauzy wing.

This other-worldly place is mine,
To stroll, for just a little while,
In idle thought and dreams divine
When twilight wears a lovely smile.

Alice Jean Do

EVENING

HUSHED is the wind in every bough
That sang all day for our delight:
The sunlit hours are past, and now
The dark clouds gather with the night.

Listen! The brown owls call again
Across our meadows, warm and dim;
Night will caress the woods with rain,
And all the shining birches slim

Will wear their jewels through the dark,
And scent the Summer night in vain –
For we shall see them not, nor hark
To the soft dripping of the rain.

Hushed is the song in every tree,
Spent is the golden day's delight,
The fields forget our steps: and we
Leave their still pathways to the night!

Glynfab John

SUMMER MAGIC

AS night's veil cools the drowsy valley,
And stars light up the heavens high,
I see a world that is undaunting,
Where gentle breezes softly sigh;
And if my hand could catch the echoes
And hide them, tightly, in my palm,
I'm sure, beneath the moonlight fanning,
No peaceful trail would lose its charm,
For perfume of the woodbine lingers,
And waving leafy trees appear
Seductive, like the essence wafting
Into the magic atmosphere.

Alice Jean Don

KATHERINE

WE see you as we see a face
That trembles in a forest place
Upon the mirror of a pool
Forever quiet, clear and cool;
And in the wayward glass, appears
To hover between smiles and tears,
Elfin and human, airy and true,
And backed by the reflected blue.

Robert Louis Stevenson

NIGHT

NIGHT, are you here again? I do not welcome you.
You have shadowed the hills and the meadows,
Folding your dark wings about the bright-eyed day.
You have summoned the bats and the hunting owl,
Called forth midsummer's moon and her attendant stars,
And brought unbidden memories to my uneasy mind.

I shall see again a girl who danced in a swirling skirt,
And remember lost friends who shared my youth and laught
I shall regret dreams that once were bright and new,
But faded and were gone like Autumn's falling leaves;
The books I meant to read, the seas I vowed to cross,
And all the signposts of my life that temped me in vain.

But I shall defy you, Night, for your reign is short;
I shall banish your sad recollections, one by one.
When they are gone I shall think of golden moments,
While slow hours pass until the moon leaves the sky.
Night, you will be vanquished by the archers of the dawn,
And I shall throw my window wide, knowing that I am free.

Peter Cliffe

SHALLOW STREAM

FEATURE of the sleepy valley,
Shallow stream you gently flow,
Winding 'neath the bending willows,
Singing softly as you go.

Smiling when you leave dark hollows
And the moon lights up your face.
Ruffled when the teasing breezes
Down your narrow course give chase.

Dreamy as the silver starlight
Dancing in the midnight blue.
Mystic, as a dark cloud passes,
Casting shadows over you.

Glowing when the silent dawning
To your mossy margins brings
Little gleams of kindled sunlight,
Stirring fishers' dazzling wings.

Alice Jean Don

DOWN BY THE SEA

THE noises that mingle,
the screams of delight,

The squark of the seagulls
forever in flight,

The promenade traffic
that grinds to a halt,

The taste on the lips
of the wind-carried salt,

The sound of the waves
that crash down on the beach,

The maverick balloon
that floats just out of reach,

The dark gipsy's parlour,
the fortunes she sells,

The fishnetty, seaweedy,
seasidey smells,

The sun on your back
and a spade in your hand,

The digging of moats
round a castle of sand,

Indelible mem'ries
on life's tapestry,

That only are manifest
down by the sea.

Brian H. Gent

THE SONGBIRD

AS Autumn shadows linger
And day comes to a close,
As shrubs prepare their vigil
For their seasonal repose;
Just listen to the songbird,
His tuneful, piping call,
A new song for the season
Before the leaves must fall.
As changing views take over
From Summer's golden day,
The songbird's cheerful warble,
Leads us, the Autumn way.

Elizabeth Gozney

THE POPLARS

THE breeze in the poplars makes music this morning:
Ah! How its sad little melody cries!
But here in the meadow the sun's brightly shining,
And the sky overhead is as blue as your eyes.

From behind a thorn hedge comes the growl of a tractor,
Almost drowning the notes of a lark's rhapsody.
The poplars stand tall and they seem to be listening
To the breeze in their branches which sounds like the sea.

The path we are taking will end at the river,
Beside an old bridge that we've come to know well.
Within its cool shade I will say that I love you;
The poplars will hear me but they'll never tell.

Peter Cliffe

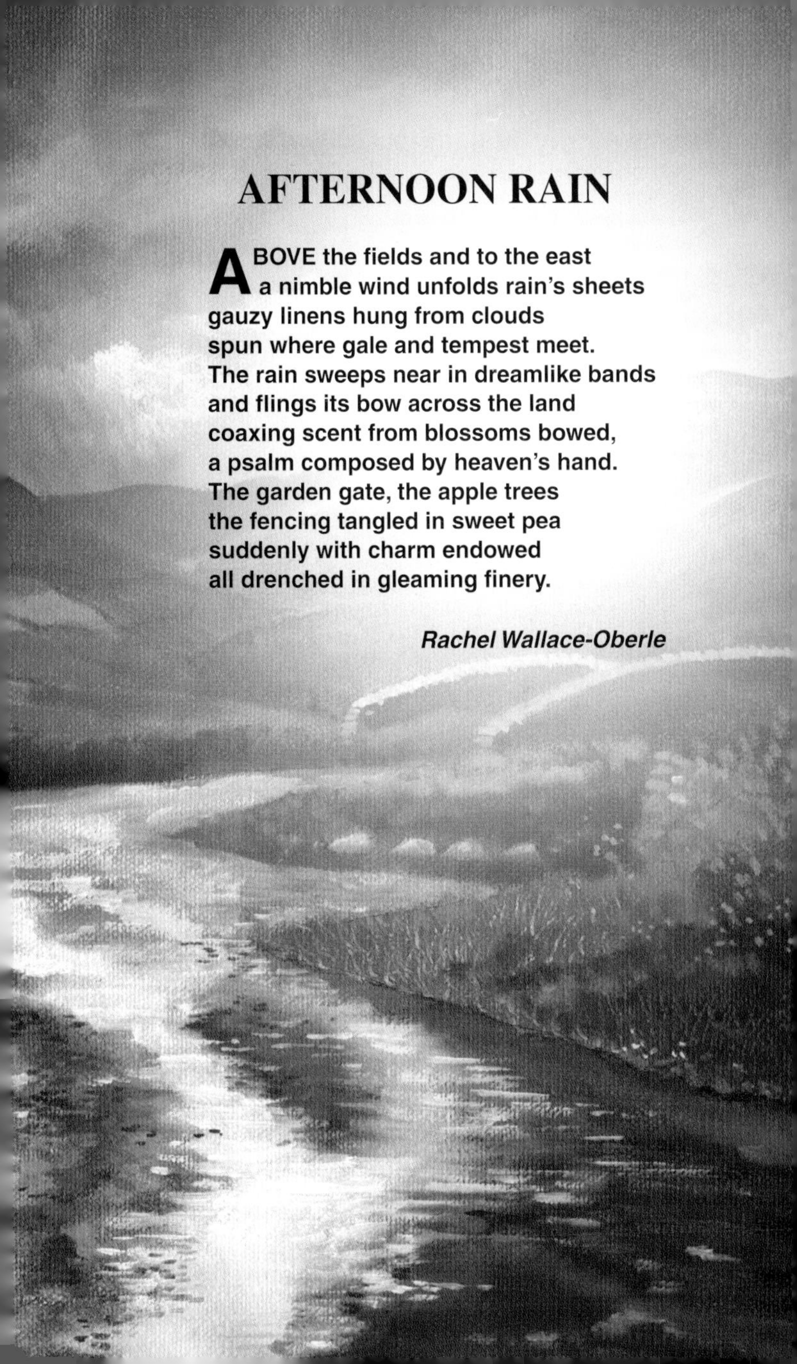

AFTERNOON RAIN

ABOVE the fields and to the east
a nimble wind unfolds rain's sheets
gauzy linens hung from clouds
spun where gale and tempest meet.
The rain sweeps near in dreamlike bands
and flings its bow across the land
coaxing scent from blossoms bowed,
a psalm composed by heaven's hand.
The garden gate, the apple trees
the fencing tangled in sweet pea
suddenly with charm endowed
all drenched in gleaming finery.

Rachel Wallace-Oberle

DAYLIGHT'S END

THE sun descends behind the hill,
As daylight softly fades,
The afterglow resplendent still,
In dark and leafy glades.

The whisper of the gentle breeze,
Night's sleepy creatures stir,
The silhouettes of graceful trees,
Etch sycamore and fir.

Owls and bats have taken flight,
Sweet quietude descends,
Enveloped in the silent night,
As once more daylight ends.

Brian H. Gent

SWALLOWS

LITTLE sister, do not sigh
Because the swallows said goodbye.
The summons came: they had to go
Before grim Winter brings the snow,
Winging over sea and strand
To settle in a distant land.

There they'll soar, so wild and free,
O'er places you may one day see,
Happy to be safe from harm
Where skies are blue and days are warm,
Wanderers a world away
From silent Autumn, cold and grey.

But they will leave when breezes sweet
Stir our meadows and the wheat,
While beneath our changeful skies
Flit the dainty butterflies;
And you will watch them from the lane,
Your swallows, when they're here again.

Peter Cliffe

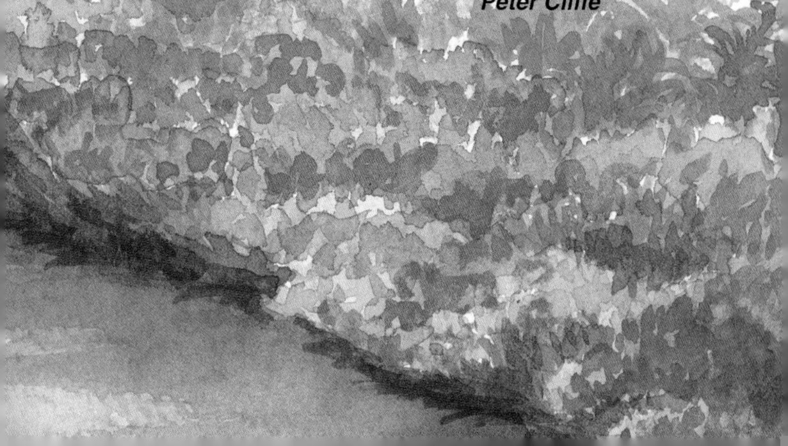

APPLE PICKING

ON ripened glowing Autumn days
I climb the pasture's sprawling fence
And wander through the fragrant maze
Of apple trees encamped like tents.
Russet globes on trembling stems
Nestled in their leafy berth
To my eager touch relent
And tumble pleasingly to earth.
Sunlit crowds of wild flowers
Fraternise with graceful ease
Nodding as I spend my hours
Contemplating apple trees.

Rachel Wallace-Oberle

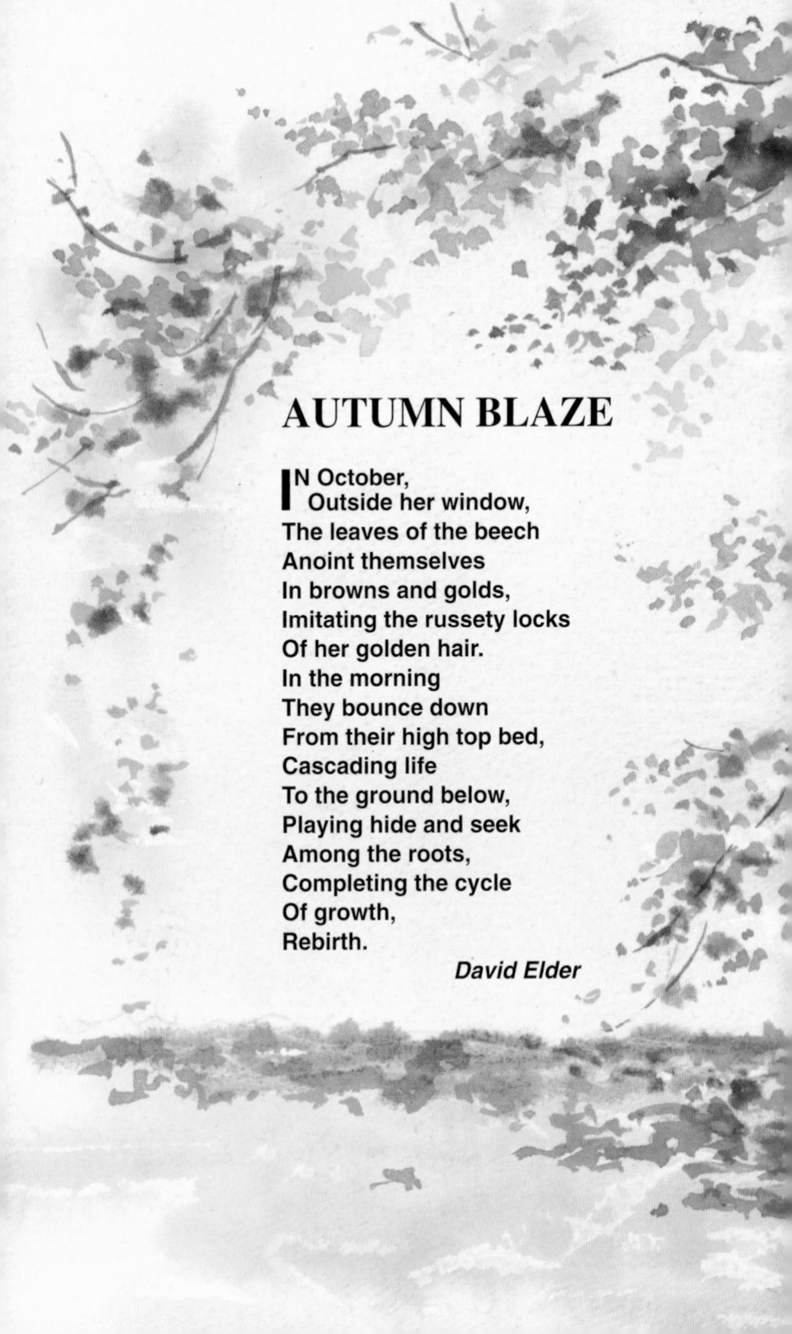

AUTUMN BLAZE

IN October,
Outside her window,
The leaves of the beech
Anoint themselves
In browns and golds,
Imitating the russety locks
Of her golden hair.
In the morning
They bounce down
From their high top bed,
Cascading life
To the ground below,
Playing hide and seek
Among the roots,
Completing the cycle
Of growth,
Rebirth.

David Elder

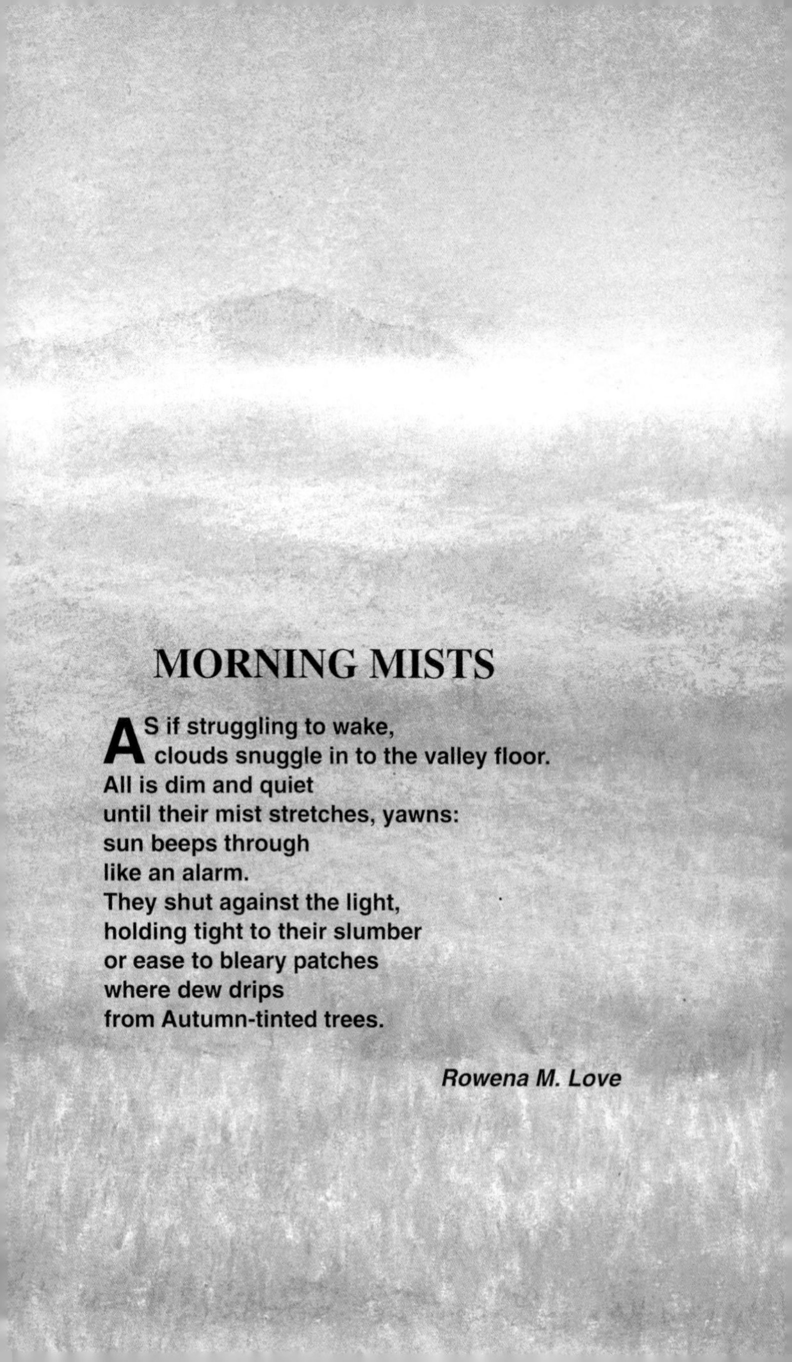

MORNING MISTS

AS if struggling to wake,
clouds snuggle in to the valley floor.
All is dim and quiet
until their mist stretches, yawns:
sun beeps through
like an alarm.
They shut against the light,
holding tight to their slumber
or ease to bleary patches
where dew drips
from Autumn-tinted trees.

Rowena M. Love

C.D. ROM
FAX

BEWILDERMENT. COM

IN this modern day and age,
Computers seem to be the rage,
You need to play your C.D. Rom,
Or contact somebody dot com,
Surf the net and don't relax,
Have a print-out, send a fax,
And when you think all help is gone,
The answer's simple, just click on,
Find it on the world wide web
And watch the 'info' flow and ebb,
For everything will be just fine,
If it's available on line;
Now this may seem a platitude
Or somewhat strange my attitude,
But, being old, I am bemused
And by the jargon quite confused,
For though it's done with great panache,
Why is oblique now forward slash?
And surely once it was the cat,
Now it's the mouse sits on the mat!
So count your pixels as you play,
For, it seems, they're here to stay,
But whilst you with the systems grapple,
On Mr Macintosh's Apple,
I'll just stay here on my own
And play my wind-up gramophone!

Brian H. Gent

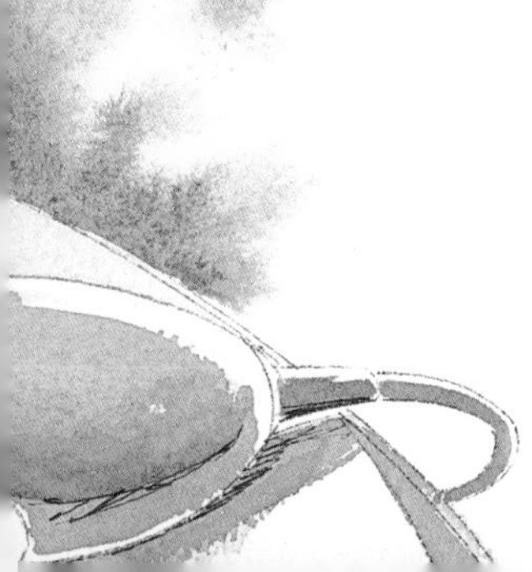

MOTHER'S PANS

WHEN I was small my mother baked
Fragrant pies and wondrous cakes
With cheerfulness and loving hands
She wielded gleaming pots and pans.
As rain or snow past windows fell
Within our kitchen's cosy spell
On tiptoe I watched Mother's jams
Simmer in her pots and pans.
Each became engraved with time
And copper bottoms lost their shine
While I went off to spread my wings
Pursuing grand and far-flung things.
On gusty days that warn of cold
My two young sons beside me hold
Spoons in eager little hands
And watch me cook with Grandma's pans.

Rachel Wallace-Oberle

FLIGHT FROM SUMBURGH

THE lighthouse pierces mist
like a knitting needle through hanks of wool;
clouds knit with shadows
in patterns as intricate as any Fair Isle.
Through their scallop lace shawl
as greys and blues of the sea's rough tweed;
its herringbone frays to waves
where it meets the mainland.
Approaching Dyce is cashmere
after homespun Shetland:
fields plain green or purled gold with harvest.

Rowena M. Love

THE STRANGER

HE walked alone along the beach.
I saw him pick an ivory shell,
caress its curving coils, until
swiftly from an outstretched arm
he threw it into spume of waves.
It fused into the blue-green haze
while seagulls cried their lonely call
and wheeled and circled out of reach.

And hidden in the dunes I knew,
or thought I knew, his solitary thoughts.
Sea-grass needled skin, sand
shifted slow beneath my feet.
Rollers swept in rhythmic crash
to dash on porpoised rocks of black.
While all the time the white birds cried
and the north wind blew.

Catherine McArdle

Hocus Pocus
SPELLS

HALLOWE'EN

WHERE have all the witches been,
Since they were here last Hallowe'en?
No doubt they sat around and cackled,
Listing all the spells they'd tackled,
Then perhaps, a cup of tea,
Made of slugs and sting of bee,
With centipedes, allowed to stew,
Makes a satisfying brew
To summon up their mystic power,
Ready for the witching hour,
Getting wicked spells in focus;
Practising their Hocus Pocus;
Broomsticks also need repair
For streamlined flying through the air.
Frogs and toads require attention
(and other things I dare not mention!).
Goblins have to go to school
To learn each new spellbinding rule,
And so obtain a Ph.D.,
In casting spells and sorcery.
But here's a fact, you never fear,
They'll all be here again this year!

With all these many chores to do,
Who'd be a witch, not me, would you?

Brian H. Gent

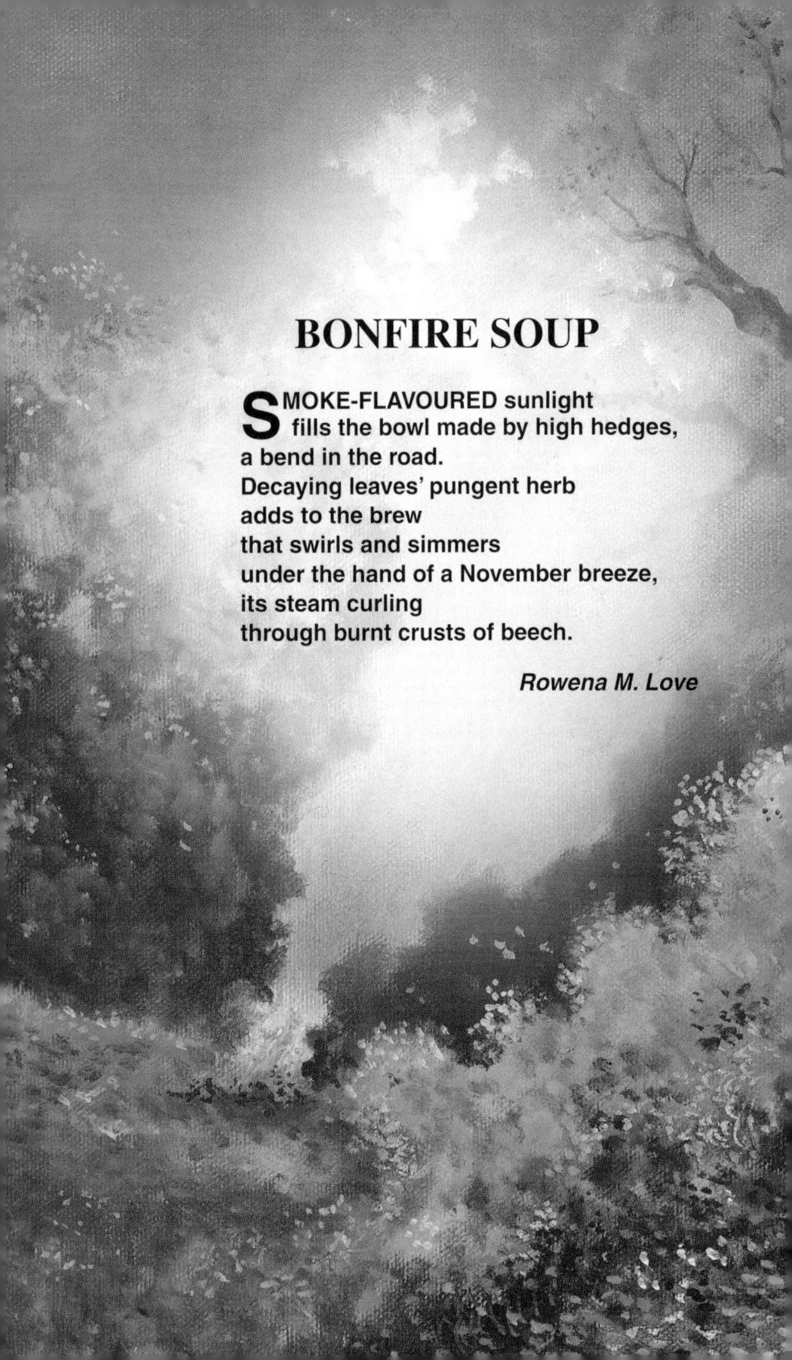

BONFIRE SOUP

SMOKE-FLAVOURED sunlight
fills the bowl made by high hedges,
a bend in the road.
Decaying leaves' pungent herb
adds to the brew
that swirls and simmers
under the hand of a November breeze,
its steam curling
through burnt crusts of beech.

Rowena M. Love

FOG

ALL is hushed, this strange white morn
No song of birds, no traffic horn
For fog has claimed the world today
Enshrouding all in softest grey
Disguising shape and muffling sound
Transforming, changing all around
Weaving spells of dark and light
Revising each familiar sight
Imparting now an eerie grace
A cobweb shawl on landscape's face
Until, at last, as day wears on
We look, and find the fog has gone
And briefly mourn the ghostly hand
That made the world a magic land.

Margaret Ingall

MORNING CATS

I WALK in unfolding morning
of frost-fresh air.
Cocoons of leaves
curl crisp in gutters,
webs hang in spangled filaments,
and cats are going home.

Hugging walls they slink
long, low and lean,
slow motion shadows,
or freeze in scupture pose
staring, unblinking,
with eyes of jewelled green.

Some cats sit at doors,
round, fat curves of cats
with twitching ears.
They play a waiting game,
those prim, proper cats
those picture-postcard cats.

Catherine McArdle

MAGIC SILENCE

A MAGIC silence fills the air,
And quietude is everywhere,
Nothing stirs in wood or tarn,
All is still in field and barn,
Save for the crunch beneath your feet,
In country lane and busy street,
So, at the ending of the day,
Our senses free to interplay,
We sit beside the firelight's glow,
Spellbound by the year's first snow.

Brian H. Gent

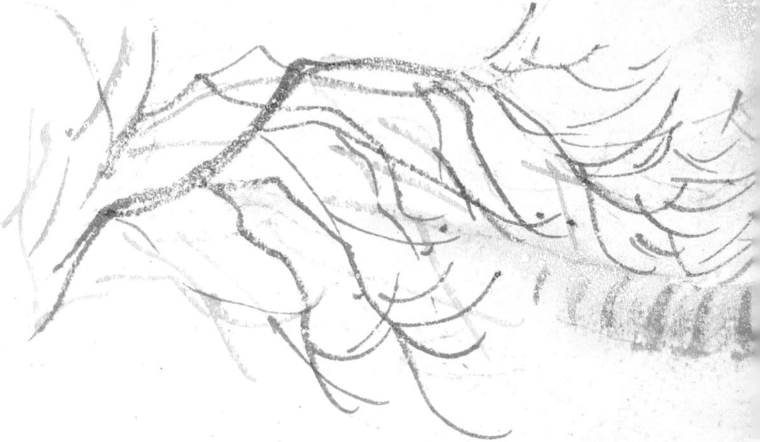

JACK FROST!

JACK FROST tiptoes secretly
Into the night,
Quietly transforming
The world into white;
As seen in the dawn
In the sun's early light:
A magical world of wonder!

Icicles scintillate,
Draping the eaves;
Cold, sparkling fern-shapes
On windows he breathes;
Upon fragile lace cobwebs,
Snow frosting he weaves —
With a garden of glittering splendour.

Where Jack Frost travels to,
Nobody knows,
But as quiet as he comes
He as silently, goes;
From his glistening white panniers,
Crisp hoarfrost he throws —
Through village and woodland to wander!

Maggie Smith

WINTER

WINTER is a vandal
stamping through the street
pinching ears and noses,
numbing hands and feet
smashing through the garden
turning green to grey
wreaking icy havoc
Winter, go away!

Winter is a wizard
weaving spells of light
painting perfect patterns
brushstrokes silver-white
fashioning the snowflakes
to decorate the day
with cold, enchanting magic
Winter, won't you stay?

Margaret Ingall

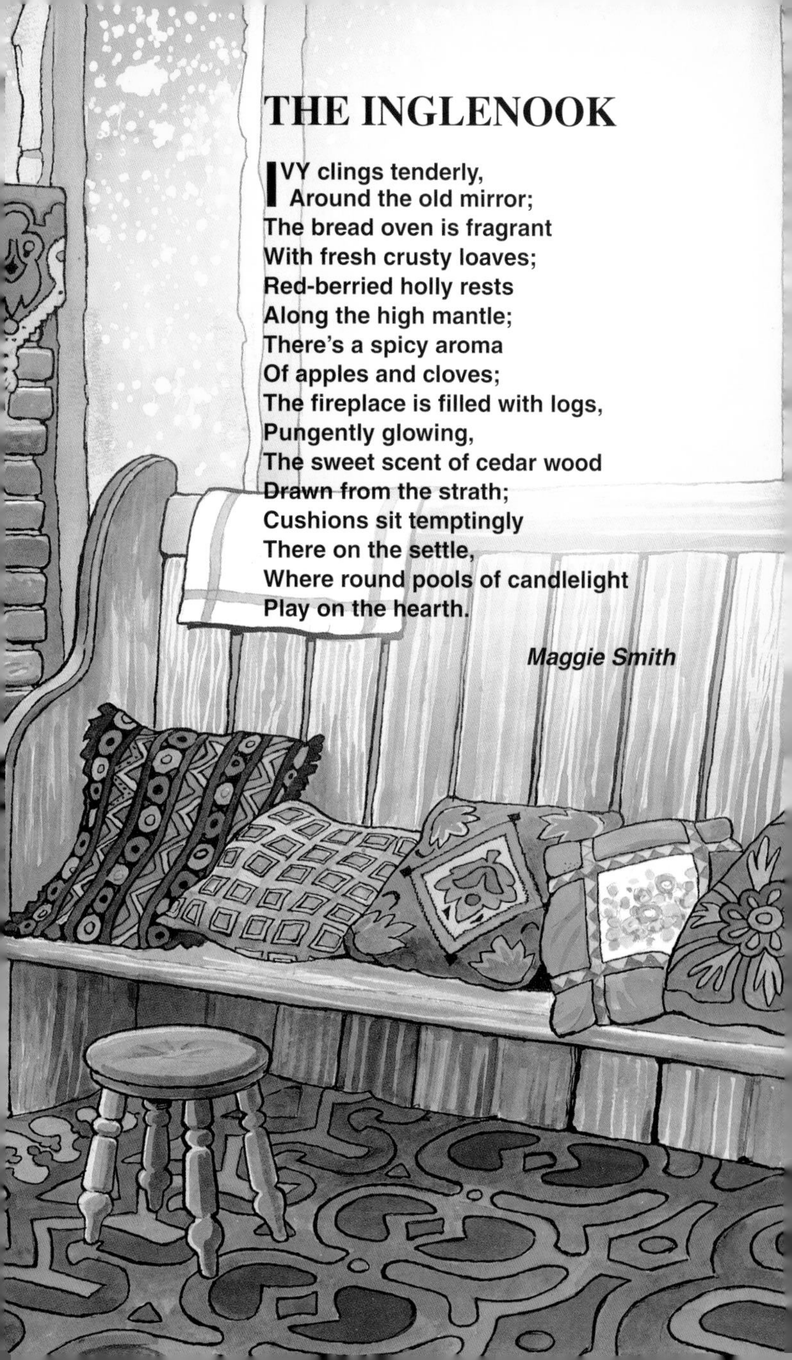

THE INGLENOOK

IVY clings tenderly,
Around the old mirror;
The bread oven is fragrant
With fresh crusty loaves;
Red-berried holly rests
Along the high mantle;
There's a spicy aroma
Of apples and cloves;
The fireplace is filled with logs,
Pungently glowing,
The sweet scent of cedar wood
Drawn from the strath;
Cushions sit temptingly
There on the settle,
Where round pools of candlelight
Play on the hearth.

Maggie Smith

CHRISTMAS TREES

BEYOND my drowsing daffodils
beneath the spell of Winter's chill
on a sweep of silvered hill
are Christmas trees.
Gathered in a stately crowd
garbed in snowfall's twinkling shroud
laden branches deeply bowed,
glad Christmas trees.
Trimmed with birds and tinselled song
lit with strings of stars till dawn
upon an icy canvas drawn,
bright Christmas trees.
And from my window to the west
throughout long months of quietness
I gaze upon their grace and bless
the Christmas trees.

Rachel Wallace-Oberle

MID-WINTER

OAK trees stand bare,
Exposed and damp,
Kept alive, just
By the drip, drip feed
Of Winter roots.

The milkman gives up
For a while
The whistling tune
Of conversation
And blows a vapour trail
On his morning round.

Yet even now
The robin sits
On garden frosted fence,
Wearing the badge
Of a beating heart
To face the dead
December dawn.

David Elder

MORNING MOON

CAUGHT between the stars and waking sun
Draped in curtains gossamer and pearled
A morning moon with glory yet unfurled
Hovers high above a stirring world
Unaware his evening work is done.

Sailing through the slowly lightening sky
Winking at the golden blush of day
The morning moon, indifferent to delay,
Acquires sleepy stars along the way
To proudly from his fading crescent fly.

Rachel Wallace-Oberle

The artists are:—

Matt Bain; Gentle Night, Daylight's End.

Sheila Carmichael; Summer Magic.

Jackie Cartwright; At Bluebell Time, Swallows, Mother's Pans, Christmas Trees.

John Dugan; King-Cups On A Barrow, She Walks In Beauty, The Lily, Hallowe'en.

Alan Haldane; Jack Frost!

Eunice Harvey; Snowdrops, Barn Owl, Morning Mists.

Harry McGregor; Evening Dusk, Evening, Shallow Stream, The Poplars.

Ian McIntosh; Wild Goose Chase, The Songbird.

Norma Maclean; The First Day, Clarsach, Garden At Twilight, Treasure!, Katherine, Apple Picking, The Stranger.

Sandy Milligan; Blackbird In Spring, Driftwood, Morning Cats.

Keith Robson; Out Of The Past, Our Village Store, Night, Afternoon Rain, Bonfire Soup, Winter, The Inglenook.

Joseph Watson; New Minted Morning.

Staff Artists; Moonlight And Dreams, Some June Day, Blow Gently, Fleeting Moments, In Twilight, Down By The Sea, Autumn Blaze, Bewilderment.com, Flight From Sumburgh, Fog, Magic Silence, Mid-Winter, Morning Moon.

JULY

S		2	9	16	23	30
M		3	10	17	24	31
Tu		4	11	18	25	—
W		5	12	19	26	—
Th		6	13	20	27	—
F		7	14	21	28	—
S	1	8	15	22	29	—

AUGUST

S	—	6	13	20	27
M	—	7	14	21	28
Tu	1	8	15	22	29
W	2	9	16	23	30
Th	3	10	17	24	31
F	4	11	18	25	—
S	5	12	19	26	—

SEPTEMBER

S	—	3	10	17	24
M	—	4	11	18	25
Tu	—	5	12	19	26
W	—	6	13	20	27
Th	—	7	14	21	28
F	1	8	15	22	29
S	2	9	16	23	30